Mindset Matters:

Daring To Hope

Simple everyday tools
to
defeat discouragement

Anne B Say

Mindset Matters: Daring to Hope

Simple, everyday tools to defeat discouragement

Cover design my Ariana Brookshier
brookshiercreative@gmail.com

ISBN-13:978-1539328995
ISBN-10:1539328996

To order more books, or to learn about the author,
please visit the author's website:
www.annebsay.com

Printed in the United States of America

DEDICATION

This book is dedicated to my Tribe.

These three couples have faithfully stood alongside me and walked out many of the truths found in this book. These women are more than friends, and more than sisters. These women are bookends in my life. I adore each one of you. At the beginning of our journey together I had no idea the joy, the love, the thrill that would permeate my life because of your presence. The men in our tribe have become much more than brothers. It has been an honor to do life with you as you circle my husband and bond together in a godly band around your wives.

To Dawn and Mike Faletti, Lori and Al Selman, Doreen and Joe Russ, and the love of my life, Terry:
Our souls have become knitted together in a way I never knew could exist. I cannot imagine doing life without you.

Thank you for daring to hope with me, and daring to hope for me.

CONTENTS

Anne B Say

ACKNOWLEDGEMENTS

I owe so much of my spiritual maturity these past few years to the **ARISE:Life Church** family. You exemplify God's family with grace and reality. In the summers before we formed as a church, you taught me how to find the heart of the Father, how to love with grace and freedom, and how to catch the dream in my heart for the fullness of Jesus in my life. It is an honor and a privilege to do life with you all.

Rhonda Fleming, owner RJF Writing Services, you are an unexpected friend and delightful joy in my life. You "get me" in ways few others do. Thank you for sharing your gifts, talents, and passions with me, in this literary endeavor, and in life. It honors me that you would lock arms with me and walk out this journey.

Theresa Harvard Johnson, somehow you make me feel like Elisha when he asked for a double portion of Elijah's anointing. But I never had to ask. You had already imparted it to me. I am incredibly grateful for you in my life, even when you are traveling around the world blessing others the way you bless me. With every piece I write, I acknowledge you.

FOREWORD

Hope is perhaps one of the most valuable assets a person can have. Without hope, there can be no progress and we can find ourselves stranded in a present that falls far short of the desires and dreams of our hearts. But when we find ourselves hopeless and discouraged, what do we do? To whom do we turn? Where can we find hope when we have none?

We have all at one time or another turned to someone for hope only to end up discouraging the very person from whom we need encouragement, attempting to convince them how bad our situation is, how nothing will ever change, how fatal it is, how horrible people are, and taking every attempt at a different perspective as a sign that they either don't understand how bad it is or don't care.

The reason for this is that encouragement or the restoration of hope is essentially an inside job. But if it is up to me to encourage me, how do I do that? How do I find hope in me when I have none?

We turn to the stories and wisdom of others who like us have struggled, overwhelmed by discouragement, and found hope. If they struggled like I am struggling now and overcame, then maybe I can, too! And Anne B. Say is just such a person. She is not a Pollyanna babbling clichés through smiling lips. Rather she is a person who has had to fight for hope. With vulnerability and strength she invites us into her battle so we can gain strategy to fight our own.

We have known Anne for some time and have watched as she has faced down fear, doubt, discouragement, even failure, with courage and wisdom. We've also been privileged to watch as she has imparted the insight she has gleaned from her trials to others and seen their lives transformed as a result.

To be brutally honest when I picked up this book, I was quite discouraged - some of it was from actual circumstances, some of it was from potential problems, some of it was from past failures, but all of it felt "real." And then I read this book. Anne challenged me and gave me tools in that moment to make a choice for hope and find it rise up within me.

None of what she writes is theory. It is all born of hard-won experience. If you will take the challenge that this book extends you, you, too, will find Anne to be an incredible guide on your journey out of the valley of the shadow of death into His Presence with fullness of joy.

Peter & Masha Oswalt
September 2016
Kennesaw, Georgia

Preface

If I could blame one thing on my slow start, of all the obstacles that held me back from following dreams, pursuing desires, and often simply having fun, I would blame discouragement as the main culprit in the mix.

There are very few things I regret in my life. After reflecting on it for a while, the one regret that might have changed things is my lack of ability to battle discouragement.

Battling discouragement could be listed in *"Everything I learned about life I learned in kindergarten."* It is as valuable as showing kindness, saying please and thank you, or learning how to tie your shoes. As adults we don't appear equipped to handle much of it in our lives. Somehow when we find ourselves in the thick of it, it seems challenging to pull ourselves out. It seems easier to just sit down and ride that slippery slope all the way into depression.

My heart for this book is that anyone struggling with discouragement would stand up tall and begin walking out of that shadowy valley. Let the tools within these pages lead you to step into your purpose and enjoy the life you were created to live.

These core values shaped this book:

- We all have seasons when we experience discouragement.
- We all have been equipped to overcome emotional obstacles.
- In Christ we have been given everything we need for life and godliness.
- We all have a unique, God-given identity.
- When we experience trials such as discouragement, God desires to be our strength.
- We can encourage ourselves when we keep in mind how far we've come.

- We are best able to navigate challenging emotions when we understand and do life from our true identity.
- We are created to be in close relationship and experience the benefits and joy of community.
- We are called to live from Christ's spirit in us,
    1. to show the world God's love
    2. to exemplify how to live victoriously in Christ
    3. to draw people to Christ by our lives

How to use this book

This book is designed to be interactive. It is designed to fuel you to move forward. The reflection questions are designed to engage you right at this moment in time, right in the place you find yourself.

The Space Between To Capture That Thought

At the end of each chapter you will find your space. This is where you can make notes, process thoughts, jot down things you want to come back to later, or just draw a picture.

The accompanying workbook is designed to take you further, should you decide to move more. Every point, every reflection, is with the intention that you will meet God there. He is always waiting. The invitation is always open. My heart and prayer is for each of us to go further, venture deeper, and reap greater blessings from this thing called our faith, our relationship with the most wonderful One I know, our Yahweh God.

CHAPTER 1
HOPE WINS

Hope is being able to see that there is light despite all of the darkness. Bishop Desmond Tutu

"Once upon a time, Satan was having a garage sale. There, standing in little groups were all of his bright, shiny trinkets. Here were tools that make it easy to tear others down for use as stepping stones. And over there were some lenses for magnifying one's own importance, which, if you looked through them the other way, you could also use to belittle others, or even one's self. Against the wall was the usual assortment of gardening implements guaranteed to help your pride grow by leaps and bounds: the rake of scorn, the shovel of jealousy for digging a pit for your neighbor, the tools of gossip and backbiting, of selfishness and apathy. All of these were pleasing to the eye and came complete with fabulous promises and guarantees of prosperity.

Prices, of course, were steep; but not to worry! Free credit was extended to one and all. "Take it home, use it, and you won't have to pay until later!" old Satan cried, as he hawked his wares.

The visitor, as he browsed, noticed two well worn, non-descript tools standing in one corner. Not being nearly as tempting as the other items, he found it curious that these two tools had price tags higher than any other. When he asked why, Satan just laughed and said, "Well, that's because I use them so much. If they weren't so plain looking, people might see them for what they were."

Satan pointed to the two tools, saying, "You see, that one's Doubt and that one's Discouragement — and those will work when nothing else will."[1]

If hope wins, then discouragement defeats.

There are various levels of discouragement. Some situations in our lives will cause us to feel discouraged for a short time. We may feel discouraged when we don't lose any weight after dieting all week, or if we got a bad haircut. These little concerns are barely noticeable, and don't cause more than a ripple in our day.

Sometimes discouragement is more forceful. It can disrupt our emotions. It is often noticeable to others around us through our actions and attitudes. Often circumstances such as bounced checks, lost sales commissions, relationship breakups, or unexpected home repairs, can leave us feeling buried under our circumstances, in the dark pit, with no obvious way out.

When discouragement becomes severe it can have debilitating effects. The stress that accompanies loss of hope can have significant physical effects, can lead to severe depression, and can shut us down spiritually. Sadly, it can even result in discouragement with God. The fallout from this intensity can cause a life to become derailed and loss of relationships and jobs to be forfeited, and tragically, even loss of life.

Hope matters.

You Have A Choice

There are certain circumstances that will lead directly to discouragement.

1. Lack of purpose
2. Lack of faith
3. Lack of results
4. Lack of support
5. Lack of vision

Did you see the key word? Lack. Discouragement is birthed where there is lack. Discouragement is birthed in a lack of hope.

Discouragement doesn't have any prejudices. Discouragement is pandemic. It reaches across countries and continents.

Discouragement ignores cultural and ethnic boundaries. It doesn't discriminate with age or gender, and it disregards financial status. It does not value of education or experience. It simply doesn't care who you are or where you came from.

Given the force behind discouragement, can we agree that discouragement is contagious? You remember the old adage, "Misery loves company." I am not a big fan of clichés. Clichés bother me because more often than not they are simply not true. I don't believe people who are discouraged and miserable always want to be around people. Some people choose to isolate rather than be around others. In addition, I believe that discouraged people can create an atmosphere where other people also get discouraged. When a person is around a discouraged individual for extended periods of time, it may become difficult to "shake it off." Somehow, emotionally, their stuff has "jumped" on others. Suffice to say here that it is important to know what is your, emotionally, and what may well be someone elses.

Every day, every hour most of us have opportunities to engage with something that feels like discouragement or at least a loss of hope for a situation or circumstance. All you have to do is turn on the news. These days we are afforded the luxury of a 24-hour news network. A few stations dedicate a "good news" hour to highlight good things that are happening, because the regular news hour reports on the scary bad stories so much. We are so inundated with stories of doom and gloom, it's easy to pick up that same emotion.

I am certainly not downgrading the struggles people experience. I am not devaluing the very difficult situations people are in the midst of. My point is that we have an overwhelming number of opportunities to encounter and/or experience discouragement every day. It's a part of life. It happens. The good news in this context is we can have tools to move through it, no matter the particulars of the situation.

Seeing The Light In The Dark

When we lose hope it is much like not being able to see in the dark. As we discovered, discouragement comes from a loss of something. When we lose hope, we can't find it, we can't see it anywhere. We need a light.

We have many spiritual ancestors who have modeled for us how to walk out of discouragement. Some did it gracefully, others needed help. God's word is for our encouragement.

All Scripture is breathed out by God and profitable for teaching, for reproof, for correction, and for training in righteousness.
2 Timothy 3:16

Where there is no prophetic vision the people cast off restraint, but blessed is he who keeps the law. Proverbs 29:11

Hope is a mindset. It is the ability to see a light in the darkness, or at least know it is there. Hope often begins with a choice. The Psalmist knew the power of the hope choice.

My flesh and my heart may fail, but God is the strength of my heart and my portion forever. Psalm 73:6

Abraham learned the power of hope. He learned the hard way, over a couple of decades. We might remember his most notable characteristic detailed in Hebrews 11:1-12, 17-19. The text is rich in hope so let's examine

> *Now faith is confidence in what we hope for and assurance about what we do not see. This is what the ancients were commended for. By faith we understand that the universe was formed at God's command, so that what is seen was not made out of what was visible. By faith Abel brought God a better offering than Cain did. By faith he was commended as righteous, when God spoke well of his offerings. And by faith*

Abel still speaks, even though he is dead. By faith Enoch was taken from this life, so that he did not experience death: "He could not be found, because God had taken him away." For before he was taken, he was commended as one who pleased God. And without faith it is impossible to please God, because anyone who comes to him must believe that he exists and that he rewards those who earnestly seek him. By faith Noah, when warned about things not yet seen, in holy fear built an ark to save his family. By his faith he condemned the world and became heir of the righteousness that is in keeping with faith. By faith Abraham, when called to go to a place he would later receive as his inheritance, obeyed and went, even though he did not know where he was going. By faith he made his home in the promised land like a stranger in a foreign country; he lived in tents, as did Isaac and Jacob, who were heirs with him of the same promise. For he was looking forward to the city with foundations, whose architect and builder is God. And by faith even Sarah, who was past childbearing age, was enabled to bear children because she considered him faithful who had made the promise. And so from this one man, and he as good as dead, came descendants as numerous as the stars in the sky and as countless as the sand on the seashore… By faith Abraham, when God tested him, offered Isaac as a sacrifice. He who had embraced the promises was about to sacrifice his one and only son, even though God had said to him, "It is through Isaac that your offspring will be reckoned." Abraham reasoned that God could even raise the dead, and so in a manner of speaking he did receive Isaac back from death.

The Apostle Paul also faced discouragement. He also had tools. He shared them throughout his letters to encourage the believers and equip them for meaningful faith journeys, no matter the circumstances. In Paul's letters to the believers in Rome, Philippi, and many other cities he describes the best tool he had: his mindset.

Paul shares these tools because they are counterintuitive to the world's culture. The power behind these mindset tools is the power of Jesus at work in us. When we align our thinking with His, we move from barely surviving to thriving.

> *Do not be conformed to this world, but be transformed by the renewal of your mind, that by testing you may discern what is the will of God, what is good and acceptable and perfect.* Romans 12:2

> *Finally, brothers, whatever is true, whatever is honorable, whatever is just, whatever is pure, whatever is lovely, whatever is commendable, if there is any excellence, if there is anything worthy of praise, think about these things. What you have learned and received and heard and seen in me—practice these things, and the God of peace will be with you.* Philippians 4:8

Mindset matters. Hope is a mindset matter.

You can't ignore the problem, but you can choose how you look at it.

You have a choice regarding the things you think about. The truth is, if we don't manage our thoughts, then they will manage us. When we set our thoughts on things that are true then we operate our attitudes and actions in the truth.

How do we know what is true?

There is a difference between what is real and what is true. Some reading this may think, *"Seriously? Real and true are synonymous."* I don't want to pick a fight, and as a lover of words I won't argue over semantics. Let's walk this out with a quick illustration.

As I stood on a platform about 40 feet above the ground. The bark of the tree was pressing into the skin on my back. I looked out along the cable and rope that stretched to the next tree and could barely breathe. The previous passes had been difficult, but this pass looked impossible. There was one cable for my feet to scoot across and a second cable above my head. The higher cable had ropes hanging from it, and the ropes were strategically placed in increasing distances apart. The challenge was to scoot along the foot cable while holding on to one rope, then reach ahead for the next rope. That was it. There was nothing more. I was more afraid than I'd ever felt before.

My fear was real. Very real. The truth, however, was different.

The truth in that particular situation was much different than what I felt. Up on that platform 40 feet above the ground I was perfectly safe. Strapped around me were yards of cords and gizmos that attached to a cable, and that cable was attached to a steel cable that ran the length of the pass between the trees. There was no possible way I was going to fall. At best, I might dangle for a moment, flying like a tree fairy until someone came and helped me put my feet back on the foot wire. The truth be told, I thought it might be a thrill to fly for a few minutes.

That day the truth was different than what was real. My emotions were very real, but they did not line up with the fact that I was completely safe. The truth was that I was perfectly safe, despite my very real emotions. You see, what is real is not the same as what is true. We can set our mind on what is true, despite what is real.

WHERE THE RUBBER MEETS THE ROAD

We get traction in our battle against discouragement when we remember what is true. When I look back over all the days, weeks, and seasons of discouragement, I realize one HUGE common denominator. I survived. What I have experienced over the decades is that there are simple, user-friendly tools that will help us get traction in order to gain victory over discouragement.

Discouragement will always leave us short in situations and circumstances. Discouragement will slow us down, drag us down, and blind us from seeing where we are going. Discouragement leaves us fumbling in the dark, but Hope is right there to turn the light on.

Hope wins. Let's begin to unpack this for our encouragement, advancement, and life enjoyment. Let's dare to hope.

REFLECTION

1. Review the three levels of discouragement shared in this chapter. Can you remember a time when you lived through one or more of these? Can you relate to the fallout of one of these levels? We will explore later how to celebrate progress, but for now, focus on the fact that you did live through it.

   If you are in the midst of a discouraging time currently, take hope. You will live through it. Read on. Be patient. Re-read the scriptures from Paul's letter to the Philippians. Think about things that are true, honorable, and just. Consider reading all four chapters of the letter, but at the very least read the following excerpt from chapter 4.

   > *Rejoice in the Lord always; again I will say, rejoice. Let your reasonableness be known to everyone. The Lord is at hand; do not be anxious about anything, but in everything by prayer and supplication with thanksgiving let your requests be made known to God. And the peace of God, which surpasses all understanding, will guard your hearts and your minds in Christ Jesus.*

   > *Finally, brothers, whatever is true, whatever is honorable, whatever is just, whatever is pure, whatever is lovely, whatever is commendable, if there is any excellence, if there is anything worthy of praise, think about these things. What you have learned and received and heard and seen in me—practice these things, and the God of peace will be with you.*

The Space Between To Capture That Thought

The Space Between To Capture That Thought

CHAPTER 2
PURPOSE

"All religions, arts and sciences are branches of the same tree. All these aspirations are directed toward ennobling man's life, lifting it from the sphere of mere physical existence and leading the individual towards freedom." Albert Einstein, Scientist, Philosopher

Where there is no vision, the people perish... Proverbs 29:18

The first tool for daring to hope is purpose. Each one of us is unique and each one of us has a unique purpose. It is a big part of our identity. It guards us against discouragement and helps keep us focused.

I grew up in a very small town in northern New York state. If you were to take a census there would be more cows than people residing there. It was delightful to grow up in this town. Everyone knew me either as my parent's youngest or Ricky's little sister. I felt comfortable and safe there.

When I was 12 we moved to a city just south of my hometown and my life changed dramatically. You see, we moved from a community of 3,600 to a bustling city of 60,000. My life also changed dramatically because my identity was defined by my role in my family. And in this new city, that was not enough.

That season began my journey of spending three decades trying to live my life (my destiny) through activity. But destiny is not about doing things. Destiny is about identity. I spent those decades finding my identity in what I was doing, instead of discovering who I was and being that person. Life is not about doing. Life is about destiny. Destiny is about identity.

It was as if I was floundering. If identity is a life ring and life is an ocean, I was drowning in the constant currents and waves. When I finally saw and grabbed hold of that life ring – my identity – hope arrived and I had purpose.

Identity and purpose are foundational for living, and they are especially powerful for defeating discouragement when it slides into our thoughts and emotions. Foundations need to be solid. They need those reinforcement bars to keep everything above it stable and functional.

Cracks, crumbling, and buckling will destroy even the most beautiful structure when they spread into the foundation. But when a foundation is strong, solid, and well-built, the beautiful things it supports function well, endure lots of activity, and most importantly, withstand storms and stand strong.

You are unique.

Your purpose is unique to you. It may look like someone else's purpose, but because of your collection of characteristics, it is definitely unique for you.

At the very basic level, you were designed and created in your momma's womb. Simply put, as you were being conceived, God was there placing your DNA, chromosomes, bones, veins, and nervous system together. It was all designed and formed at conception.

For you formed my inward parts;
you knitted me together in my mother's womb.
I praise you, for I am fearfully and wonderfully made.
Wonderful are your works;
my soul knows it very well.
My frame was not hidden from you,
when I was being made in secret,
intricately woven in the depths of the earth.
Your eyes saw my unformed substance;
in your book were written, every one of them,

the days that were formed for me,
when as yet there was none of them. Psalm 139

This text applies to everyone. It includes those with physical disabilities, cognitive challenges, crossed eyes. It includes albinos, redheads, and people with six toes, cleft palates, and my silly pinky toenails. God takes the time to personally design every single human being.

Even Job in all his discomfort and misery, acknowledged that God created him.

Your hands fashioned and made me Job 10:8

God took special pains with you and me. He did it with a plan in mind. As He knit you together he thought about who you would grow up to be. God had a plan for you at the moment you were conceived, and that plan is still in play.

For we are his workmanship, created in Christ Jesus for good works, which God prepared beforehand, that we should walk in them. Ephesians 2:10

It would be pointless for there to be a purpose for our lives and us be unable to figure it out. When we are struggling with discouragement, the first light in the darkness is to discover, find, or maybe remember our purpose.

WHERE THE RUBBER MEETS THE ROAD

It's about *all* of you.

There is so much more to you than your physical appearance or your IQ. What makes you who you are includes all of you. The best part of you is that you are an ever-growing version of yourself. Discovering purpose is not only a tool that will help you walk out of a discouragement mindset, it will also begin to expand who you are. You begin to grow into the bigger, better version of yourself. It's about your insides and your outsides.

Consider this graphic. You are made up of these and more!

Let's take a minute and look briefly at some of these.

Passions. In addition to your physical appearance, your cognitive abilities, and the color of your hair, you also have passions. Each one of us has things in our life that move, excite, and motivate us. Passions are placed in our hearts at that "designer" moment. They are key clues to our identity and help us determine our purpose.

Abilities. Remember that you were designed to be exactly the way you are. Abilities are part of our DNA. They are those things that we do naturally. I have the ability to eat, write, and paint with my right hand. I am not left-handed, nor am I ambidextrous. I do not have that same ability with my left hand. My husband does not have flexibility. No matter how hard he tries, how much he practices, he simply cannot touch his toes. Abilities also include the ability to sing on key, sing in a particular octave, tone-deafness, colorblindness, etc. Abilities allow us to do particular things, and they prevent us from doing particular things.

Because I do not have the ability to sing, I will not find my identity in leading worship at my church. I will not find my passion singing opera or in a country rock band. It does not prevent me from singing, however it does give me clues to my identity and those Ephesians 2:10 works that God has prepared for me beforehand.

Skills. Your skills are another important part of your identity.

Skills and abilities speak volumes about us. They connect us with others as we learn them, as we find our vocation around them. Skills don't just happen. They are learned. We learn how to cook, we learn how to speak another language, we even learn how to brush our teeth effectively.

For years I wasn't much of a cook, but in the past 10 years I have developed a few culinary skills and actually enjoy something I used to dread. I was not born with the ability, and it did not come naturally to me. I had to learn this skill.

Since skills are learned, they have to be learned somewhere. Those places would be our experiences. The longer we live, the more experiences we have. Our skills are closely tied to our experiences. Our experiences are another significant part of our identity.

Experiences. Family experiences might include traveling a lot, or they might include rarely leaving one's hometown. Educational experiences might include struggles learning, or earning a PhD. It might include extra-curricular sports, theater, or clubs. Work experiences impact our identity as well as church experiences. The list can go on, but the point is God wants to use your experiences to help shape your purpose.

Being mindful of our experiences helps us keep our eyes on our purpose and off the things that are stealing our joy and leaving us in that pit of discouragement. God doesn't waste a thing. He won't waste anything you have experienced. He wants to redeem all of it for Himself and His kingdom.

Personality Patterns. Personality patterns are not designed to put people in a box. They are designed to help us understand ourselves so we don't get into confused ruts, so we can appreciate our own giftings and those of others.

Here's where I get passionate. Back in the 90's when I was teaching high school I took some workshops on learning styles. They changed the way I taught and the way I approached my students. Later I encountered personality patterns and fueled these passions even hotter. Since then I have led many work teams and small groups to a more clear understanding of who they are and how God created them to be.

Communication Styles. Communication styles are also a part of our identity. Communication is a dynamic part of relationships and life. Understanding how we communicate, how we take in information and how we express ourselves is essential to having successful relationships in all parts of life. Miscommunication causes more problems in our world than any other single issue.

Understanding how we process information and make decisions helps us better understand ourselves. When I look back over the years of my adult life I am able to follow the trail between how I processed information and why I made certain decisions.

When we add this piece called communication to our purpose puzzle we increase the clarity with which we explore our purpose. It gives us more clarity into who we are and that helps us understand our those Ephesians 2:10 good works which we were created for.

Bucket List Dreams. Finally, let's touch on bucket list dreams. Bucket list dreams are a bit different than our heart passions. Heart passions can be more closely related to values, such as family, helping single moms get their lives stabilized. They can also be things that get your heart pumping. Things such as designing, organizing, performing are heart passions.

Bucket list dreams are those things we pursue and achieve, or at least they are things we long to pursue and achieve. They include things to do, things to be, and things to get. Bucket list dreams come out of that place in your DNA where God put the seeds the deepest inside you. They are valuable and well hidden. They are treasure and to be searched out and found. And they are significant indicators to our identity and our purpose.

Our experiences may have overshadowed our dreams, but they are still there. I know this because I have experiences that have buried them so deep that I didn't think I had any. But God… But God knew they were there and He worked them to the surface, even though I didn't understand.

"God had a dream, and wrapped your body around it." Lou Engle

"[Dreams are] seeds of possibility planted in your soul, calling you to pursue a unique path to the realization of your purpose." John Maxwell

The beautiful part of all this is that the world needs each one of us. We will dig deeper into this later, but for now embrace the all of you.

REFLECTION

1. Think about the categories we explored in this chapter. What do you really like about yourself in each of these? What are the things you wouldn't change about you? Spend some time, and don't give up. You will find something when you look deep enough.

   - Physical appearance
   - Passions
   - Skills and abilities
   - Experiences in life
   - Personality patterns
   - Communication styles
   - Bucket list dreams

   Where is there tension in some of these areas? Make some notes and begin to get some clarity on your identity. It will help develop your unique purpose.

The Space Between To Capture That Thought

The Space Between To Capture That Thought

CHAPTER 3

STRENGTHEN YOURSELF IN THE LORD

"Therefore, as you received Christ Jesus the Lord, so walk in him, rooted and built up in him and established in the faith, just as you were taught, abounding in thanksgiving." Colossians 2:6-7

"Have I not commanded you? Be strong and courageous. Do not be frightened, and do not be dismayed, for the LORD your God is with you wherever you go." Joshua 1:9

I had been out in the country visiting a friend. I had some things stored in her barn and I walked out through the field to check on them. While I was there the weather shifted, a monstrous summer storm started and the rain, thunder, and lightning let loose. That was about all I needed that day. In the midst of the cacophony of thunder bangs, and the wind, and the rain, my own tears began to fall and my own wails roared along with nature's.

A few weeks later on a warm summer day I was sitting on the porch enjoying my coffee and doing my bible study. It had been a long season of finding myself and finding peace. To be honest, I was tired. I was discouraged. I was beginning to think that God had forgotten about me. There had been a tsunami in Asia and I was fairly certain that God had gone to the other side of the world to do relief work. As I gathered my things on the porch, I still felt drained and barely functioning better than on autopilot. I needed strengthening.

In my foggy fatigue, I struggled with my things and they began falling to the floor at my feet. As I watched, one single index card slid out from the pile and lay separate right in front of my eyes. On it was a single verse.

But he said to me, "My grace is sufficient for you, for my power is made perfect in weakness." Therefore I will boast all the more gladly of my weaknesses, so that the power of Christ may rest upon me. 2 Corinthians 12:9

In my season of weakness, God had met me. There was no chastising or scolding for not being a more capable adult. There was only an invitation. God was inviting me to let Him be my strength. It was a mindset change.

It may seem fairly obvious, but the reason we need strengthening is because we are feeling weak. The Apostle Paul understood weakness and strength. The words in his letter to the believers in Corinth two thousand years earlier spoke to my soul and encouraged me.

God was *not* on the other side of the world doing tsunami relief work. He was right there with me, and now I could see that. It was another step in defeating my discouragement.

Some of us are highly capable. For the most part, we can do life very well on our own. For much of my life I was this way. To be honest, I was quite proud of the fact that I could navigate through obstacles, challenges, and storms quite well. Maybe I was a little too proud of myself.

Eventually we all experience the mother of all storms. Eventually we all encounter a circumstance where we recognize our own mortality and determine that we need help. I had reached that point during that season. I knew I couldn't do this one on my own.

Personally, I think Jesus is the best friend I've ever had. He always shows up when I need Him. (He promised to never leave, so He is always there.) Jesus is the best because He always has what we need. All those things we need come through the third member of the Trinity, the Holy Spirit.

You are stronger than you think

Jesus gives us the Holy Spirit for several reasons. Jesus gives us

His Spirit so that we can do more than we are capable of doing on our own. The Holy Spirit is described by many names. Here are some:

- Breath of God (John 20:22)
- Comforter (John 15:26)
- Counselor (Isaiah 11:2)
- Advocate/Helper (John 16:7)
- Seal (2 Corinthians 1:22)
- Intercessor (Romans 8:9-11)
- Spirit of Truth (John 14:17)
- Teacher (John 14:26)

When discouragement slides in and we need strengthening we have what we need to "strengthen ourselves" in the Holy Spirit. The Holy Spirit was given to us to comfort us when we need comforting, to help us when we need help, to intercede for us when we need prayer, essentially to strengthen us when we are discouraged. The Holy Spirit is here to meet your needs when you are feeling:

- Lack of strength
- Lack of vision
- Lack of confidence
- Lack of security

You have everything you need.

We have everything we need to do this life. This truth was one of the most difficult for me to grasp during that very difficult summer. When I looked around me, it didn't seem like I had everything I needed. As a matter of fact, all I could focus on was what I didn't have.

And that is exactly the point. I was looking in the wrong place. I kept looking further into the darkness instead of looking at the light in the darkness. The truth of God is that with His Spirit in us we have the fullness of Him in us. Therefore, by default, we have everything we need.

His divine power has granted to us all things that pertain to life and godliness, through the knowledge of him who called us to his own glory and excellence, 2 Peter 1:3

Isn't is crazy? We have everything we need, yet discouragement is spreading in epidemic proportions around the world.

One terrific example of someone who knew what to do when discouragement invaded his mind and heart was David in the Old Testament. David was named king years before he took the throne. Nevertheless, even before his anointing, we can see where David had opportunity to encounter discouragement. Based on the text in 1 Samuel, David's own father treated him more like a hired hand than a son.

Then Samuel said to Jesse, "Are all your sons here?" And he said, "There remains yet the youngest, but behold, he is keeping the sheep." And Samuel said to Jesse, "Send and get him, for we will not sit down till he comes here." 1 Samuel 16:11

Throughout his life, David had many circumstances and situations which he navigated the same way. He managed discouragement by strengthening himself.

Now David was greatly distressed... But David strengthened himself in the Lord." 1 Samuel 30:6

David, known as the man after God's own heart, was greatly distressed on more than a few occasions. David had all the right stuff. He was humble, he was handsome. He was faithful when no one was looking, and he knew his identity. Life is equal and fair when it hands out opportunities for discouragement. The difference in people is how they handle it. David was anointed king. He experienced many challenges before he took the throne, and he encountered many more afterwards. The key is how he responded to the discouragement. No matter what, David knew what to do.

He strengthened himself in the Lord.

He is our role model for identity and purpose, and for how to strengthen ourselves in the Lord.

WHERE THE RUBBER MEETS THE ROAD

When we are discouraged, distressed, or defeated we need strengthening because we feel weak. The word "strong" used in 1 Samuel 30:6 is worth a closer look.

Beginning with the original language, which is Hebrew, and the grammar, we can see that David is the one giving himself strength and the one receiving the strength. That may look a bit confusing until we dig a little deeper.

The word "strong" is the Hebrew word "chazak." It is often used in describing the strength one thing has over another. When David strengthened himself, he overpowered the emotions that were dominant, and established himself in a position where he knew he could function again.

When an emotion such as discouragement has the dominant place in our thoughts and hearts, it leaves us in a trajectory leading us from frustration to anxiety to fear. Consistent pressure over time is what propels us further down that trajectory. In the end it leaves us paralyzed and stuck, not being able to see that light in the darkness (Hope Wins chapter).

When we strengthen ourselves in the Lord we do things that give ourselves strength. We take control hold of our anxiety. When we have a grip on our discouragement in our thoughts and our emotions, then we can begin to repair ourselves with the only thing that will be strong enough to last: the Lord.

Discouragement, and its relatives fear and anxiety, live in that darkness and work to keep us from finding the light. They are significant indicators that we are off track somewhere. We find the light by going back to the Lord and examining where we got off track and take the necessary steps to get back on the right track. In our context we began with purpose. That is always the best place to begin when we have to reestablish ourselves.

David's habit was simple. He always began by acknowledging how he felt, what he was facing in the circumstances. Then he reminded himself of God's ability and willingness to meet him in the circumstances. He reminded himself of God's character. He sang, danced, and rejoiced in the faithfulness of God. David didn't quit until he was strengthened.

What does it take to keep dancing until you are strengthened? What does it take to keep worshipping until you feel God in your mind and heart? Let me assure you, whatever it takes, *you have it*. You have everything you need. It's in your decision to do it. It's in the choice you make to begin and not quit until God strengthens you.

People worship in a variety of ways. Personally, I enjoy the variety. I enjoy the contemporary songs that are simple and have repeat phrases because it gives me a specific thought to focus on before the Lord. But other times I am deeply moved by the ancient hymns, all for the same reason; I focus on the Lord. The one thing that needs to be consistent in worship is the Object of our attention.

Worship can also happen in scripture reading, in journaling, in dance, and instrumental music. Worship is simply focusing on the Lord in a particular area. Worship strengthens us in the Lord because it reminds us of who He is. It puts the situation and circumstances in the perspective of His point of view. The same happens with scripture reading, journaling, etc. It strengthens us because it settles our mindset back in the truth of who God is even in the midst of all we are facing. It is a huge tool in defeating discouragement.

Hezekiah is another example of someone who brilliantly strengthened himself in the Lord. Hezekiah was king when Israel was being badgered and bullied by some aggressive neighbors. As king, Hezekiah is growing frustrated and discouraged. In addition the people are discouraged. Finally, in all the frustration (discouragement), he takes the most recent nasty-gram and heads to the temple.

Hezekiah received the letter from the hand of the messengers, and read it; and Hezekiah went up to the house of the Lord, and spread it before the Lord. And Hezekiah prayed to the Lord: "O Lord of hosts, God of Israel, enthroned above the cherubim, you are the God, you alone, of all the kingdoms of the earth; you have made heaven and earth. Incline your ear, O Lord, and hear; open your eyes, O Lord, and see; and hear all the words of Sennacherib, which he has sent to mock the living God. Truly, O Lord, the kings of Assyria have laid waste all the nations and their lands, and have cast their gods into the fire. For they were no gods, but the work of men's hands, wood and stone. Therefore they were destroyed. So now, O Lord our God, save us from his hand, that all the kingdoms of the earth may know that you alone are the Lord."
Isaiah 37:14-20

Hezekiah was tired. He was tired of the incessant battering from the enemies of Israel. The people of Israel were tired. They had been taunted, bullied, and watched the Assyrians take out surrounding nations. Their God had been mocked and they had been mocked. Enough was enough.

Have you ever become tired of the obstacles and circumstances and even people who work tirelessly to disrupt your life and rob your peace? This text paints a very real picture of what the nation of Israel was feeling. It's a picture with an emotion many of us can relate to.

... as when children come to the moment of birth and there is no strength to deliver them. Isaiah 37:3 NIV

Discouragement can leave us feeling like there is no more strength to go on. The first time I read this story about Hezekiah I read it like a recipe. It was as if God was giving me the how to's that I needed to get through my discouraging season. It was the light in the darkness that helped me find my way.

Here is how I see it played out in my mind's eye.

Hezekiah was the leader of God's chosen people. He was aware of the people's emotional state. He was also aware of God's position. I can see Hezekiah looking out the palace window at the people, then looking at the letter in his hand. I can see his lips purse; his eyes narrow. In one motion, Hezekiah takes a deep breath and turns on his heels. The muscles in his jaw are flexing and his free hand alternates between open and fist-like. Out the door and crossing to the temple, Hezekiah marches with his arms swinging and his robe lifting off the ground behind him. He barely notices the people as they make way for him to pass. He barely notices the Levi priest as he enters the temple and heads for the alter. Hezekiah's heart is filled with righteous indignation against the Assyrians and Israel's enemies. His heart is also filled with reverence for Jehovah, the God of Israel.

At the altar Hezekiah spreads out the letter and falls to his knees.

Hezekiah knew how to handle discouragement. He knew where his strength lay and made it a priority to go there first. Strengthening ourselves in the Lord is a necessity in defeating discouragement. The process is simple. Why is it so hard to do?

When we are discouraged, the hard part is remembering to step into this place. It is as if it goes against our nature. In one sense, it does. Discouragement is self-focused. It looks at our circumstances and ourselves and accepts defeat. Hope is Lord-focused. The best way to strengthen yourself in the Lord is to be with the Lord.

David, Hezekiah, and many others in the Bible show us simple, effective ways to strengthen ourselves when we are discouraged. It all begins with being with the Lord.
1. Remember who He is.
2. Remember what He has promised to do.

3. Acknowledge our own efforts, weaknesses, and shortcomings.
4. Confess any sin that Holy Spirit brings to mind.
5. Ask Him for help. He promises to help when we ask.
6. Remember some of His promises.

That is how we strengthen ourselves in the Lord. That is how we begin to defeat discouragement.

That discouragement feeling haunted me much of that summer years ago. That feeling like I haven't the strength to get the job done permeated many of my days. As I walked back into the kitchen that day, Jesus showed up in my life and gave me the hope I desperately needed. My body was as tired as my soul. As I stepped into the kitchen my foot caught on the door threshold. I stumbled and dropped my journal and index cards. As they slid to the floor everything stayed intact except for that one index card slid out of the notebook and lay directly in front of me. Let's read it again.

> *"My grace is sufficient for you, for my power is made perfect in weakness." Therefore I will boast all the more gladly of my weaknesses, so that the power of Christ may rest upon me. For the sake of Christ, then, I am content with weaknesses, insults, hardships, persecutions, and calamities. For when I am weak, then I am strong."* 2 Corinthians 12:9-10

My knees buckled and I found myself prostrate on the floor, physically, emotionally, and spiritually. In a very literal sense, Jesus had to bring me to my knees in order to teach me how to be strong. That was day #1 in the lesson of a lifetime. Strengthening myself begins on my knees.

REFLECTION

1. Consider an area of your life where you are discouraged, or can be prone to discouragement. How are you currently strengthening yourself in the Lord? What does that look like for you?

After reflecting on your typical process, review how David and Hezekiah strengthened themselves. The goal is to create a better process for strengthening yourself in the Lord.

Review the 6 steps (page 42-43). Begin now for yourself.

Here are some verses to help you.

Fear not, for I am with you; be not dismayed, for I am your God; I will strengthen you, I will help you, I will uphold you with my righteous right hand. Isaiah 41:10

Instead of your shame there shall be a double portion; instead of dishonor they shall rejoice in their lot; therefore in their land they shall possess a double portion; they shall have everlasting joy. Isaiah 61:7

Now to him who is able to do far more abundantly than all that we ask or think, according to the power at work within us. Ephesians 3:20

And endurance produces character, and character produces hope, Romans 5:4

And my God will supply every need of yours according to his riches in glory in Christ Jesus. Philippians 4:19

For I know the plans I have for you, declares the LORD, plans for welfare and not for evil, to give you a future and a hope. Jeremiah 29:11

"Blessed is the man who trusts in the LORD, whose trust is the LORD. He is like a tree planted by water, that sends out its roots by the stream, and does not fear when heat comes, for its leaves remain green, and is not anxious in the year of drought, for it does not cease to bear fruit." Jeremiah 17:7-8

The Space Between To Capture That Thought

The Space Between To Capture That Thought

CHAPTER 4

CELEBRATE PROGRESS

The celebration of success overshadows the challenges that were encountered along the way. Jeffery Benjamin

Several years ago I joined a weight loss program. At the time it was exactly what I needed and it helped me a great deal. The end result was I lost 30 pounds and kept it off.

One of the reasons this program was successful for me was the tracking system. Each week I tracked my food intake, and each week I weighed in. The weighin was huge. I could see how much weight I'd lost that week, and what my total weight loss was. Most weeks I'd lost something, but there were weeks when I'd gain a pound or stay the same. Regardless of the weekly outcome, I would celebrate my progress, either weekly or overall. The celebration was part of the journey.

My weekly celebrations included a phone call to my mother, who would cheer me on in that wonderful way mothers do. When I lost increments of 5 pounds, I would get a charm for my key ring, a sticker for my chart, and everyone would clap for me. To be honest, I liked the affirmations, and I liked the charts. Even if you don't like charts, it is still important to celebrate the little steps you take toward a goal, especially when it comes to defeating discouragement.

When all the nation had finished passing over the Jordan, the Lord said to Joshua, 2"Take twelve men from the people, from each tribe a man, 3and command them, saying, 'Take twelve stones from here out of the midst of the Jordan, from the very place where the priests' feet stood firmly, and bring them over with you and lay them down in the place where you lodge tonight.'" 4Then Joshua called the twelve men from the people of Israel, whom he had appointed, a man from each tribe. 5And

Joshua said to them, "Pass on before the ark of the Lord your God into the midst of the Jordan, and take up each of you a stone upon his shoulder, according to the number of the tribes of the people of Israel, 6that this may be a sign among you. When your children ask in time to come, 'What do those stones mean to you?' then you shall tell them that the waters of the Jordan were cut off before the ark of the covenant of the Lord. When it passed over the Jordan, the waters of the Jordan were cut off. So these stones shall be to the people of Israel a memorial forever." Joshua 4:1-7

You are making progress.

Knowing how far we've come is important. We have all come far. The fact that you are still breathing means you are still on your journey. If you're like me, you have experience with obstacles, and you have experience with overcoming a few. It's the ones we have overcome that we need to focus on.

When things go slow. There are times in our lives when the process to get where we want to go becomes drudgingly slow. On my weight loss journey there was a time when many weeks went by and I didn't lose a pound. It was during those weeks I was grateful for that tracker to remind me how far I'd come. I was grateful for those silly, little charms on my key chain. They reminded me of the journey and helped me not give up. When progress gets slow and seems to stop altogether, we need to be able to celebrate our progress. When we take the time to celebrate how far we've come we become a little more energized, a little more motivated, a little more focused, and often we are able to see new strategies and ideas we hadn't thought of before.

When things get tough. Celebrating progress will encourage you when things get tough. How many situations do we encounter in life when we think it's just not worth it to go on. When I was on my weight loss journey and hit that dreaded plateau, I often thought of giving up. I'd already lost 25 pounds, wasn't that good enough? It was hard and all my efforts seemed in vain since I wasn't losing any more weight. When it got hard, remembering how far I'd come helped me keep going.

This tool kept me on track. I'd never dieted so significantly before. I'd never worked so hard on my health before. It was a new journey for me, and keeping my progress and my goal in mind kept me going. Ultimately, it helped me be successful.

When things aren't working. There are also seasons in our journey when what we are doing doesn't appear to be working. Tracking your progress and celebrating your successes in the little steps helps you measure what is working and what isn't. It helps you keep your power on and monitor what is effective and recognize when you simply need to hang in there.

My weight loss journey was more about perseverance than anything else. There have been times in my life however, when celebrating the progress meant encouraging myself when things got dark and I couldn't see the light. (See chapter 1.) Sometimes when it's dark and we can't see our way forward, looking back at how far we've come can be enough for us to see the light. It can motivate us, bring a bit of hope, help us take a deep breath and take another step forward.

The Old Testament history is full of celebrations.

Shabbat is a weekly celebration that emphasizes rest from physical work. The purpose of Shabbot is to allow us to rest and refresh ourselves. This time is to celebrate our work and celebrate God, who gives us the ability to work and enjoy the fruits of our labor. Genesis gives us the principle for our Shabbot rest.

> *And on the seventh day God finished his work that he had done, and he rested on the seventh day from all his work that he had done. So God blessed the seventh day and made it holy, because on it God rested from all his work that he had done in creation.* Genesis 2:2-3

Passover is the first of the three major festivals. It has historical and agricultural importance. Historically, Passover commemorates the exile and the ultimate freedom from the Egyptian captivity. Passover also represents the commencement of the harvest season.

The name "Passover" refers to the story in which God "passed over" the houses of the Jews when he was slaying the firstborn of Egypt in the last of the ten plagues.

During the celebration of the Passover Seder, the matzah, unleavened bread, is made without leaven, consisting only of flour and water, baked quickly. This is in remembrance of the hastily prepared bread the Jews baked as they fled Egypt.

Are you beginning to see why celebrating is important? It was important to God, and He also encourages us to make it important. Let's look deeper at the Passover celebration. Everything about the Seder meal is significant.

- Charoset – chopped walnuts, wine, cinnamon and apples representing the mortar the Jewish people used to assemble the Pharaoh's bricks while enslaved
- Chazeret – horseradish to reflect their bitter affliction
- Karpas - potatoes, onions, or parsley are dipped in salt water, remembering the bitter tears they shed
- Betza – egg is metaphoric for two reasons. As an egg hardens as it boils, so did the people of Israel strengthen their commitment as their situation became more challenging the situation. The roundness of the egg also symbolic of the cycle of life.
- Zro-a – bone shank symbolizes the sacrificial lamb offering
- Maror – romaine lettuce is also to remember the bitter affliction of slavery

Rosh Hashanah is the Jewish New Year. It is a time to celebrate the creation of the world. The traditions and rituals of Rosh Hashanah are very different from the current New Year celebrations. There is no partying, fireworks, or football games. Instead, this is a time for reflection and self-evaluation. This reinforced the notion of responsibility for our life, conduct, and actions.

Yom Kippur is the holiest day in the Jewish year. Its principle focus is atonement combines repentance and confession through fasting and prayer. Yom Kippur celebrates the atonement. The sacrifice had been made, and sin is covered, so the celebration is joyful, hopeful, and future-oriented.

There are other celebratory holidays, festivals, and feasts in the Jewish tradition. The point is, marking our progress, especially out of difficult and dark times, is powerfully beneficial to our progress forward. It keeps discouragement at bay and hope in our hearts and minds.

WHERE THE RUBBER MEETS THE ROAD

We celebrate so many things in our culture. We celebrate births and birthdays, weddings and anniversaries, promotions and retirements. We celebrate sports victories, the first day of school, and graduations. We are a culture that likes to celebrate.

What if we began to celebrate our progress?

On my weight loss journey I chose to celebrate my progress. It helped me be successful and fend off discouragement. The means of celebration was very specific. Going out for a big meal that included indulging in a fancy dessert was not an option. It would have been counterproductive. I would have found myself back in that dark discouragement the next day, emotionally and physically. I was no longer used to eating that way, and it wasn't helpful.

I chose ways to celebrate that kept me encouraged. I chose ways to celebrate that were fun, but not expensive. I kept the big ticket celebrations for my final hoorah!

REFLECTION

1. What situation is currently bringing you discouragement?
    Can you look back and track some progress you've made?

    Re-read the story in the beginning of this chapter from
    Joshua 4:1-7. Make note of how God encouraged the nation
    of Israel to make memorials. Pay attention to why they
    needed to do this. If you can, go back in your mind and
    make some memorials.

    What would our lives be like if we made memorials for the
    times we overcame, for the times we made small steps
    forward? What would our homes look like if we had
    keepsakes from these moments? Momentos from these
    God-encounters in our dark days?

    Use the blank pages that follow to get creative with this
    process. I give you permission to go wild and celebrate! It
    just may become a new, terrific tradition.

The Space Between To Capture That Thought

The Space Between To Capture That Thought

CHAPTER 5
GATHER YOUR TRIBE

Call it a clan, call it a network, call it a tribe, call it a family: whatever you call it, whoever you are, you need one. Jane Howard

Find your tribe. Love them hard. Ashley Forrer

It was December 2014 and my husband and I were meeting with another couple. All four of us were hungry for small group community but couldn't find the blend of intimacy and faith and worship we were craving. We did the only thing we could think to do. We met in a small room in our church, on our knees, in a circle, and we prayed.

You can be close.

Each of us asked the Lord for names of people who were hungering like we were. We desired a group of people with whom we could be family. On our wish list were things like:

- Fellowship in worship
- Scripture study
- Fellowship over a meal
- Spiritual growth in each of us
- Intimacy
- Trust
- First responders to each other

We prayed for an hour or so. We repented from things that came before the Lord in our hearts. We asked for Him to lead, direct, and bring people with desires like ours. Then we each wrote down the names we heard.

Sometimes it's scary to do things that put God to the test. I don't make a practice of it, but when I have, I've seen Him do some things that have made my head spin. On this particular morning, as we finished our time of prayer, we put our lists out in the circle to read the names.

On each piece of paper there were common names. There was a peace around those names, and a smile on our faces. We planned a dinner for the next weekend.

WHERE THE RUBBER MEETS THE ROAD

What is a tribe? Merriam-Webster offers three simple definitions[2]:

1. a group of people that includes many families and relatives who have the same language, customs, and beliefs
2. a large family
3. a group of people who have the same job or interest

We wanted to be a group of people who share a common desire to know God more deeply, to allow His presence through the Holy Spirit to move in and through us, and to develop intimate, family-like relationships with each other.

We have been meeting weekly for 2 years now. We have learned to trust each other. I heard once that trust is a decision. We had to learn to decide to trust each other with our blemishes and brokenness. As we tested the process, we gained confidence.

While trust is a decision, confidence comes with experience. Each of us has grown our own confidence in each other and in the group as a whole. Are we perfect? Oh my no, not by a long shot. But we are learning some things we could only learn in a tribe.

First, we are learning how to be vulnerable with who we are and what is going on in our lives. We were beginning to understand that we could only grow in our relationship with God if we are able to be honest with Him. If we could learn by being honest and vulnerable with each other, it might help us be honest and vulnerable with each other. Isn't it ironic that it is so hard to be honest and vulnerable with God, and yet He already knows everything about us? Isn't it hard to imagine that He is patiently waiting for us to tell Him what He already knows?

One of the ways I grew in my relationship with the Lord in this area was by growing in my relationships with those in my tribe. As I was willing to be honest and vulnerable with them, I was more able to be honest and vulnerable with God. In both, I was strengthened when I needed to face and overcome challenges such as discouragement and the fear of failure.

The second important dynamic I am learning in my tribe is to love all of a person, the good and the bad, just as Jesus loves us. This has been on my personal wish for over 15 years. Just when I think I have figured out how to love all of a person, another person shows up and challenges me again.

In our little tribe, we are not perfect. But if we are going to grow in the ways we desire to grow and mature, we have to learn to love each other the way Jesus loves us: completely, quirks and all.

Tribes are a huge part of defeating discouragement, and they have a great deal of value in all these other ways. As you think about a tribe, who they are, how you do life together, when and where, keep an open mind and allow God to create a picture, allow Him to tweak that picture, and most of all, allow Him to breathe life into that dream.

One of the interesting dynamics of our little tribe is how different we are, and yet our common desires unite us. In this interesting dynamic, I have learned more about the unique characteristics of God in each of us. It reinforces our identity and helps us understand Him more.

Another dynamic about our tribe that brings great value is how they see me more as God sees me, especially when I'm struggling.

My tribe has spoken life into me in those times when I was discouraged and ready to give up. They reminded me of who I am and what my dream is. They prayed for me and over me. Their words and actions loved me back on my feet and helped me reconnect with my Father to strengthen myself (chapter 3).

This didn't just happen. It required me to trust them with my thoughts and emotions. It required me to speak up about the fears and frustrations I was facing. This is the power of a good tribe. It didn't happen overnight, and it didn't happen by chance. It happened with intention and purpose, both in the group commitment to trust, and in their commitment to love.

Life with God reminds us that we need a few people in our lives with whom we have that closeness in our relationships.

There are many messages in the media that will tell you that you can do things alone, that if you "need" others you are weak, but along you are strong. On the surface that may seem true, but when discouragement and frustrations are challenging you, when the storm begins to rage, you need people who know you, who love you, who have your back, and who will help you get through.

REFLECTION

1. Have you ever been in a group with a intentional intimacy? What made it work? What would you change if you re-grouped or formed a new group?

2. Have you ever thought about a tribe-like group? Who would you include? Use The Space Between to dream about the who, the how, the different ways you might be able to develop intimacy.

3. What might prevent you from forming or joining such a group? Many of us have trust issues, and many of us have been able to work through them. Be encouraged, you can too! (Note: Consider going through the accompanying workbook for a more in-depth response to this deeper issue.)

The Space Between To Capture That Thought

The Space Between To Capture That Thought

CHAPTER 6
CULTIVATE COMMUNITY

I can do things you cannot. You can do things I cannot. Together we can do great things. Mother Theresa

The world is a dangerous place, not because of those who do evil, but because of those who look on and do nothing. Albert Einstein

I grew up with a significant void in my identity. What identity I did possess was either shallow or wrong. I can remember my shallow identity sounding like this:

- *Chatty Cathy* – because I would visit the neighbors and talk a lot.
- *Annie-Poo* – because I was the youngest.

Over the years these pieces of whimsy became identity statements that sounded a lot like:

- I don't have anything of value to say.
- I am not smart enough to have a conversation.
- I am not wanted, they just have to take care of me.

Over the years they became stronger because they were reinforced by circumstances. Like all our thoughts, they continue to grow outward in the direction they face. Our thoughts, like trees, grow bigger as we "feed" them. Positive thoughts grow into positive thought patterns and negative thoughts grow into negative thought patterns. They are reinforced regularly as we process life daily. Each conversation, each situation, and every circumstance we find ourselves in reinforces our thought patterns. Our thought patterns become what many refer to as "self-fulfilling prophecies.

The good news is that we get to choose which way our thought patterns grow. And it's important that we do exactly that.

Negative thought patterns that are based on frustration, fear, and anger emotions have significant impact on our health. Dr. Caroline Leaf is a cognitive neuroscientist with a PhD in Communication Pathology who specializes in Neuropsychology. She discloses the impact of these negative thought patterns internally on our DNA, and our immune system, and externally on our attitudes and actions.[3]

My incorrect interpretation of my identity growing up developed into a strong belief system that left me feeling discouraged and defeated both in my personal life and also in my professional life. It took years before I understood myself and my place in community. It was a journey, but it was the best trip I've ever taken.

Our identity directly impacts how we see ourselves fitting into the communities around us. When we allow circumstances and other people tell us who we are, we never develop a true sense of belonging. This can occur in our families, our workplaces, our neighborhoods, our social networks, even our churches.

Understanding our identity correctly leads to more positive thoughts which grow into positive thought patterns. Those thought patterns directly drive your attitudes and your actions. When the foundation in your mindset concerning where you belong in community is strong, you defeat discouragement.

You belong.

Beyond the Tribe is the Community. The Tribe is a safe place. It is a place where close friends can hold you true to your unique, God-given identity. It is the people who help you find and maintain your purpose. The Tribe keeps you from falling victim to discouragement.

Community is where you live that purpose out to its fullest.

It took some time for me to focus on myself and realize my identity was based on a cracked and crumbling foundation. As I asked God for help, He delivered. I met people, encountered resources, and found safe places (tribes) to process my thoughts. As I broke free from the negative thought patterns that had grown into lies which held me back, I began to experience freedom. My heart and spirit were filled with a joy I'd never experienced before. Discouragement was no longer an option. As I grew in my understanding of who I am and what I was created to do, I developed purpose and peace.

Before community can be cultivated, we must understand what it is and where we fit.

The simple definition of community from Merriam-Webster states that community is a group of people who live in the same area (such as a city, town, or neighborhood).[4] Another way to look at community is grammatically. "*Com*" means with, and "*unity*" means what it states, unity. Community literally means "with unity."

There are many definitions and types of community. For the purpose of this context, we are focusing on how we can cultivate community as a tool to defeat discouragement.

Over the recent months, years, and even centuries, we have seen communities of people rally together over an issue, a crisis, or a specific need. That is the purpose and point of community: to come together and bring ourselves, do what we are capable of doing (see chapter 2), and accomplish a purpose.

There are several tools we use to help people discover their unique identity and develop a sense of purpose. In chapter 2, Purpose, we unpacked a few of those tools. Those are the same tools we will use to find our place in community.

The Bible gives us encouragement in the context of community. We know that God made each of us uniquely. Just like snowflakes, there is only one you. Only you have your DNA. Only you have your combination of experiences, abilities, passions. Not a single part of who you are is by accident, and all of it is for the purpose of knowing God more intimately and bringing who He is to the world around you. That world is your community. The Apostle Paul made a beautiful analogy in his letter to the Romans.

> *For by the grace given to me I say to everyone among you not to think of himself more highly than he ought to think, but to think with sober judgment, each according to the measure of faith that God has assigned. For as in one body we have many members, and the members do not all have the same function, so we, though many, are one body in Christ, and individually members one of another.* Romans 12:3-5

Each one of us has a place in community. Each one of us has a purpose and a "job" designed to bring us fulfillment in life and in our relationships, beginning with our relationship with God.

I love the way Romans chapter 12 begins, with the mindset. How we think of ourselves, and how we think of others. Remember, what we believe dictates our thoughts, and our thoughts drive our attitudes and actions. When we understand our purpose, our identity, our place in community, then we live with peace, freedom, and in hope.

Paul explains it again to the believers in Corinth.

> *For just as the body is one and has many members, and all the members of the body, though many, are one body, so it is with Christ. For in one Spirit we were all baptized into one body—Jews or Greeks, slaves or free—and all were made to drink of one Spirit.*

> *For the body does not consist of one member but of many. If the foot should say, "Because I am not a hand, I do not belong to the body," that would not make it any less a part of the body. And if the ear should say, "Because I am not an eye, I do not belong to the body," that would not make it any less a part of*

the body. If the whole body were an eye, where would be the sense of hearing? If the whole body were an ear, where would be the sense of smell? But as it is, God arranged the members in the body, each one of them, as he chose. If all were a single member, where would the body be? As it is, there are many parts, yet one body.

The eye cannot say to the hand, "I have no need of you," nor again the head to the feet, "I have no need of you." On the contrary, the parts of the body that seem to be weaker are indispensable, and on those parts of the body that we think less honorable we bestow the greater honor, and our unpresentable parts are treated with greater modesty, which our more presentable parts do not require. But God has so composed the body, giving greater honor to the part that lacked it, that there may be no division in the body, but that the members may have the same care for one another. If one member suffers, all suffer together; if one member is honored, all rejoice together. Now you are the body of Christ and individually members of it.
1 Corinthians 12:12-27

Our culture is inundated with messages that tell us we can do this life alone. We see movies about the lone ranger types who are able to take down the bad guys all by themselves. The truth is that we are relational beings. We were created for relationship, by a triune God who lives in relationship. There are many parts of life that we can only navigate, glean from, grow from, and especially live from which can only happen in community. It is in our DNA.

Community is a necessary defense against discouragement.

WHERE THE RUBBER MEETS THE ROAD

Cultivating community is an ongoing tool in defeating discouragement. As with the other tools, we keep them handy for those moments when we need them.

Cultivating community means finding your place. In order to find you place, you must know your identity and purpose. You need that solid foundation as you step out and explore the land we call community.

You have a place.

God designed us uniquely to fit together in a body, a group of people. We each have a special place, and we each have a special function we are designed to perform. It is not robotic, nor is it automatic. But we were created to live together in community and do our part to keep the community healthy and thriving.

The text in 1 Corinthians 12 equates our part in community with a body. A body has many parts, externally and internally. Each part has a function, and each function is vital to the overall health of the body. No one part is more or less important to the body. Each one is necessary. One of my favorite examples in the human body are those little hairs inside our noses. As small and unbecoming as they may seem, they play a very important role in our body's health. Those little hairs collect dust and other irritants and prevent them from entering our lungs and respiratory system. Those little hairs are important to our body as a whole. Can the body survive without them? Well, yes, but it will put more pressure than necessary on the respiratory system and the immune system. And when those two systems can't handle the overload, the body gets sick.

In the same way each person in community is necessary. No matter how insignificant a role a person may play, they are important to the community as a whole. As we discover our identity and our purpose, we begin to catch a vision for our place in our communities. As we explore our passions and allow God to reveal to us dreams that exist in our hearts, that vision develops more detail and clarity.

More than once in my life I have moved to a new part of the county. One of my moves took me to live in Spain. As a young woman in a foreign country, it took a lot of effort to "find my place." In the more recent moves I was able to navigate and find my way largely due to understanding these parts of myself, and finding the places I fit in.

When I moved back to Atlanta nearly a decade ago, I already had much of this hard data about myself and my identity. Shortly after I got settled in, I began the venture and discovered there were several social groups with some of my same interests. It was relatively easy to get connected and find my place.

As I've grown more into my identity (a journey which I believe lasts a lifetime), that vision for my purpose has become more clear. There are some basic principles which are keys to navigating this journey well.

First, purpose can vary widely. God allows limitations to guide us as we walk with Him. As a young woman some of these include financial limitations and experience limitations. As a young mom, and especially as a single mom, financial limitations were significant. Other limitations during that season were time limitations and physical limitations. God uses these seasonal limitations to guide our seasonal purpose. Today, as an empty-nester and a married woman who is also retired and available to pursue dreams and passions with greater effort, I have different limitations. Those same ones from my single mom years look vastly different.

My place in community as a retired teacher, now author and speaker, has a different focus than as a single mom. It's no less important, it's simply different.

Second, abilities and skills grow. As I changed careers, took more educational classes my skills increased. Through my journey of weight loss I discovered the ability to cook. Most recently I have opted to make many of my own personal care products.

Because of these changes, my passions have ebbed and flowed, and I now enjoy connecting with others who have need or interest in cleaner eating and cleaner skin care. My place in community has ebbed and flowed with these life seasons.

A final key is experiences. This is an area that many of us miss because we discount experiences, we hide our shameful experiences, or we want to forget our embarrassing experiences. The truth is that God never wastes anything with us, and that includes our experiences.

My experiences as a single mom give me greater empathy for single moms. That empathy gives me a place in my community. I can, and do, create opportunities to connect with them, to be a support and a bookend for them. Without understanding my experience I would miss this significant part of me and community.

REFLECTION

1. Spend some time with the Lord reflecting on your purpose, abilities and skills, and experiences. Review chapter 2, Purpose, and begin to dream about how you might take your place in your community, right now in this season. Consider journaling regularly as you process this in greater detail.

2. If you have a tribe, or even a tribe-like person or two, meet with them and have some intentional conversation about the topic of purpose and community. See where the discussion leads. It may make room for some creative ideas!

The Space Between To Capture That Thought

The Space Between To Capture That Thought

CHAPTER 7
NOT THE END OF THE STORY

We will always have circumstances that challenge us. There will be temptation to be discouraged, to give up and pack it all in. Take a moment and remind yourself of the statements scattered throughout this book.

You have a choice.

Hope is a mindset matter.

You are unique.

You are stronger than you think.

You have everything you need.

You are making progress.

You can be close.

You belong.

Now go back and look at some of the scripture truths that resonated with your heart and mind. Find some you can focus on to encourage you and help you keep your hope on.

You have a choice. You can choose hope. Hope wins. Always.

Thank you for sharing this journey with me. I pray you will continue to encounter the One in whom we place our hope.

It all changed for me when I began to understand who I am in God's eyes, was able to embrace my past as something God could use and, with all these pieces of "me," dare to dream about the future. When I got there, I knocked down discouragement. When it tries to get back up, I am now better positioned to give it another kick.

I was 22 years old before I knew I had a sense of humor. Today, laughing is one of my favorite things to do. My husband and I value laughter. It keeps us from taking ourselves too seriously. It reminds us that God is truly in control, and He desire us to be joyful.

For many years my love of laughter was processed in my mind as immature and silly. Those thoughts kept me from bringing fun into many areas of my life and into many relationships. Discovering my love of laughter set me free.

Another area that brought me identity freedom was when I realized that my past could be used to help others find freedom. Our experiences, all of them, can be redeemed to be ways to connect with people. God never wastes anything in us or in our lives. This does not mean we have to reveal the muck in public, but we can use these experiences to help us empathize with others who are still stuck and looking for breakthrough.

One other way I found helpful in believing in my identity was in the way I communicate. The way we process information and the way we express ourselves is a big part of who we are. It enriches our communication with others, and it helps us manage our own mindset as we make decisions and manage our lives.

We are better equipped to defeat discouragement when we know our purpose and place in community. We know our purpose and place when we know our identity. At that point we can begin to explore our passions and dreams for our lives.

This is not an overnight process. We spend weeks with people in small groups just to get them to a place where they can begin to dream. It takes thought, managing our mindsets, and trial and error. But we find the greatest contributor to the process is the tribe.

REFLECTION

1. Take a moment and reflect on your passions, abilities, and experiences. Give yourself permission to just reflect, without pressure or expectation. Consider it a first step in a safe place.

   When you do something with all your heart you experience

   - Enthusiasm – because you love it
   - Effectiveness – because you're good at it
   - Excellence – because you give it your best, you desire to excel

2. Now consider your abilities. What kinds of skills do you have? Be honest. Be real. You have skills! They may be organizing and cleaning, design or construction, or cooking, counseling, or teaching.

3. Finally, reflect on your experiences. Take your time, and begin with easy, non-emotional ones like education, travel, and vocation. Then reflect a bit on relational and spiritual experiences. God never wastes anything!

   Please note: If you have traumatic experiences in your life, please consider finding a safe, godly counselor with whom you can process some of them. God always desires to redeem them. He invites us into the process by bringing them to Him, working through forgiveness (toward others and ourselves), and exchanging them for something more beneficial.

NOTES

CHAPTER 1

[1]HTTP://WWW.INSPIRATIONALARCHIVE.COM/137
9/SATANS-GARAGE-SALE/#IXZZ4IKLFEXK1

CHAPTER 5

[2]HTTP://WWW.MERRIAM-
WEBSTER.COM/DICTIONARY/TRIBE

CHAPTER 6

[3]HTTP://WWW.DRLEAF.COM

[4]HTTP://WWW.MERRIAM-
WEBSTER.COM/DICTIONARY/COMMUNITY

ABOUT THE AUTHOR

Anne B Say is a recognized author, speaker, and coach who helps women discover and live into their unique God-given identity. Her passion is to make identity and purpose real, and to equip others with the tools to live that out.

Anne's use of metaphors to tell a story and impart a principle help others understand God's truth in a way that is often described as "where the rubber meets the road". She weaves personal experiences and metaphors that help others make sense of who they are and how their relationship with God can bring greater clarity and focus into their lives.

Anne is a wife, mother, step-mom, grandmother (Mimi), step-grandmother, retired teacher, struggling gardener, and avid reader. She loves to laugh, sing, be outside, watch movies, and hand out with her adorable husband, Terry.

Topics Anne regularly speaks about:

- Building a solid foundation in your identity
- Make up your mindset
- How to turn an embarrassing past into a worthy future
- Where life and faith collide
- Daring to count it all joy
- Putting up fences, tearing down walls

Other books by Anne:

- Seasons of Change, an interactive journal for growth
- 7 Things You Must Do To Be Happy (ebook)

You are invited to connect with her at:
http://www.AnneBSay.com.

Made in the USA
Charleston, SC
03 February 2017